Fun with ABCs

Nivel Hills Publishing

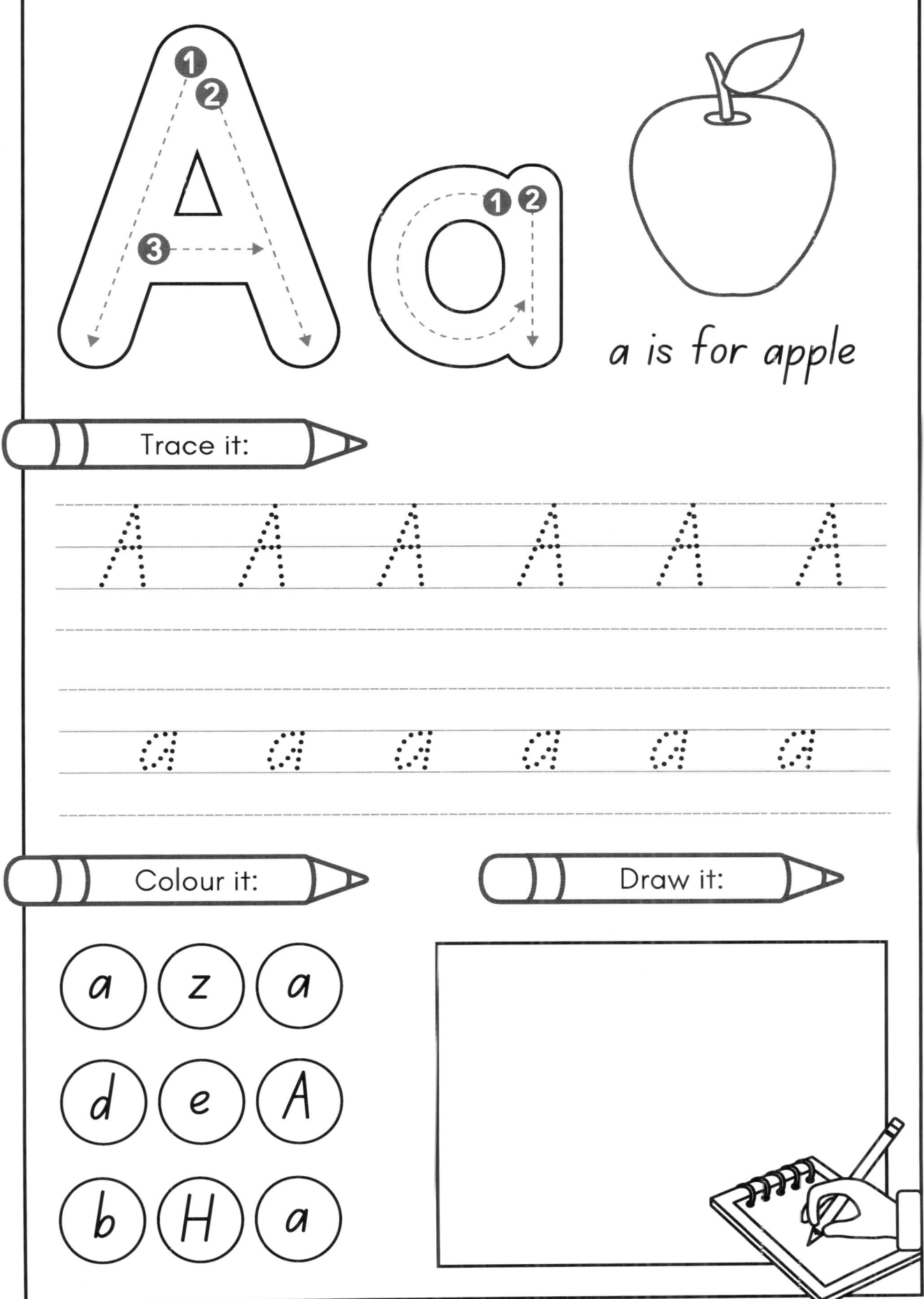

A a

a is for apple

Trace it:

A A A A A A

a a a a a a

Colour it:

a z a
d e A
b H a

Draw it:

b is for bird

Trace it:

B B B B B

b b b b b b

Colour it:

b D d
w q B
b d a

Draw it:

C c

c is for cake

Trace it:

c c c c c c

c c c c c c

Colour it:

e   y   i

c   v   C

k   R   s

Draw it:

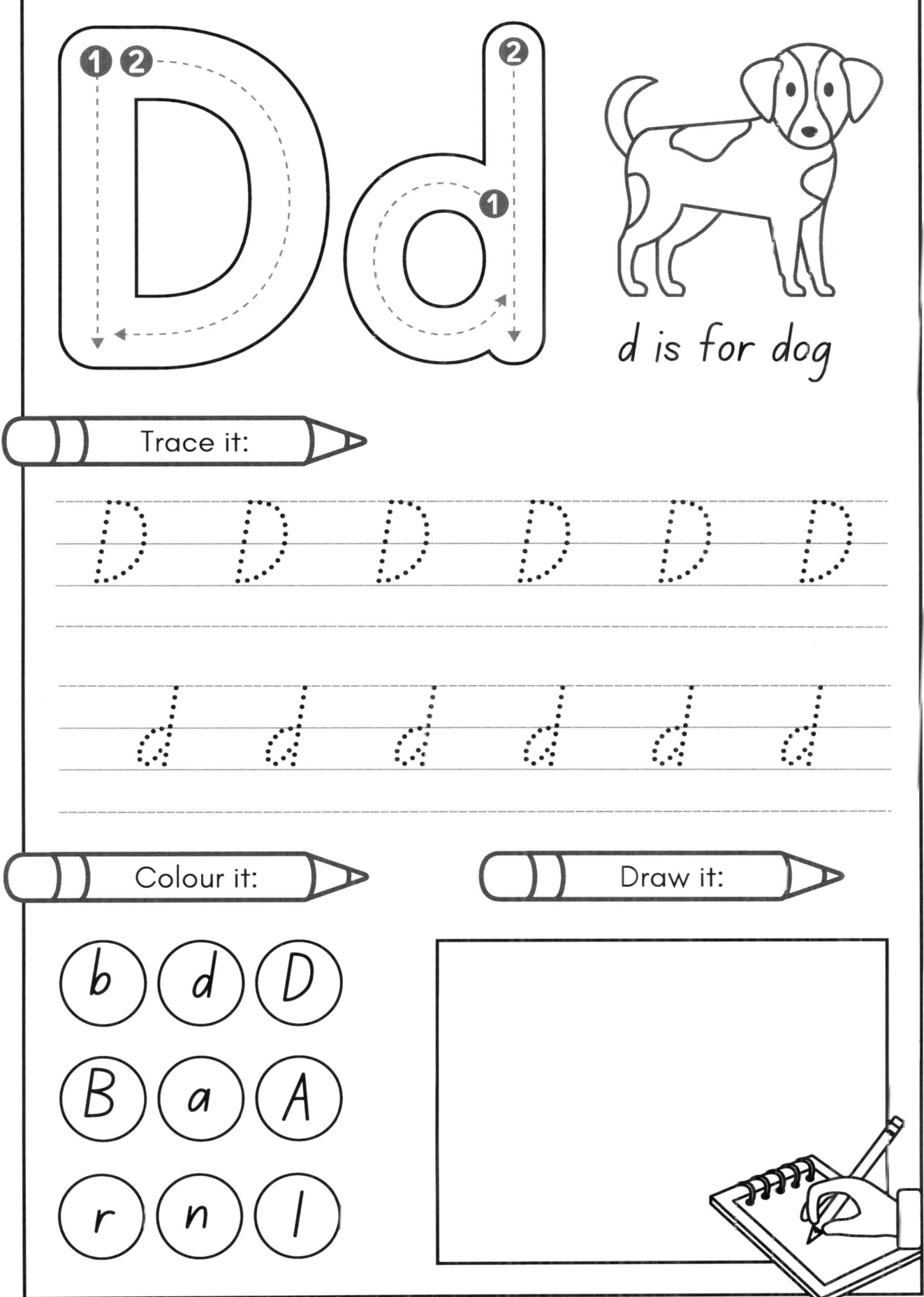

Dd

d is for dog

Trace it:

D D D D D D

d d d d d d

Colour it:

b d D

B a A

r n l

Draw it:

E e

e is for elephant

Trace it:

E E E E E E

e e e e e e

Colour it:

f e e

E r T

o p j

Draw it:

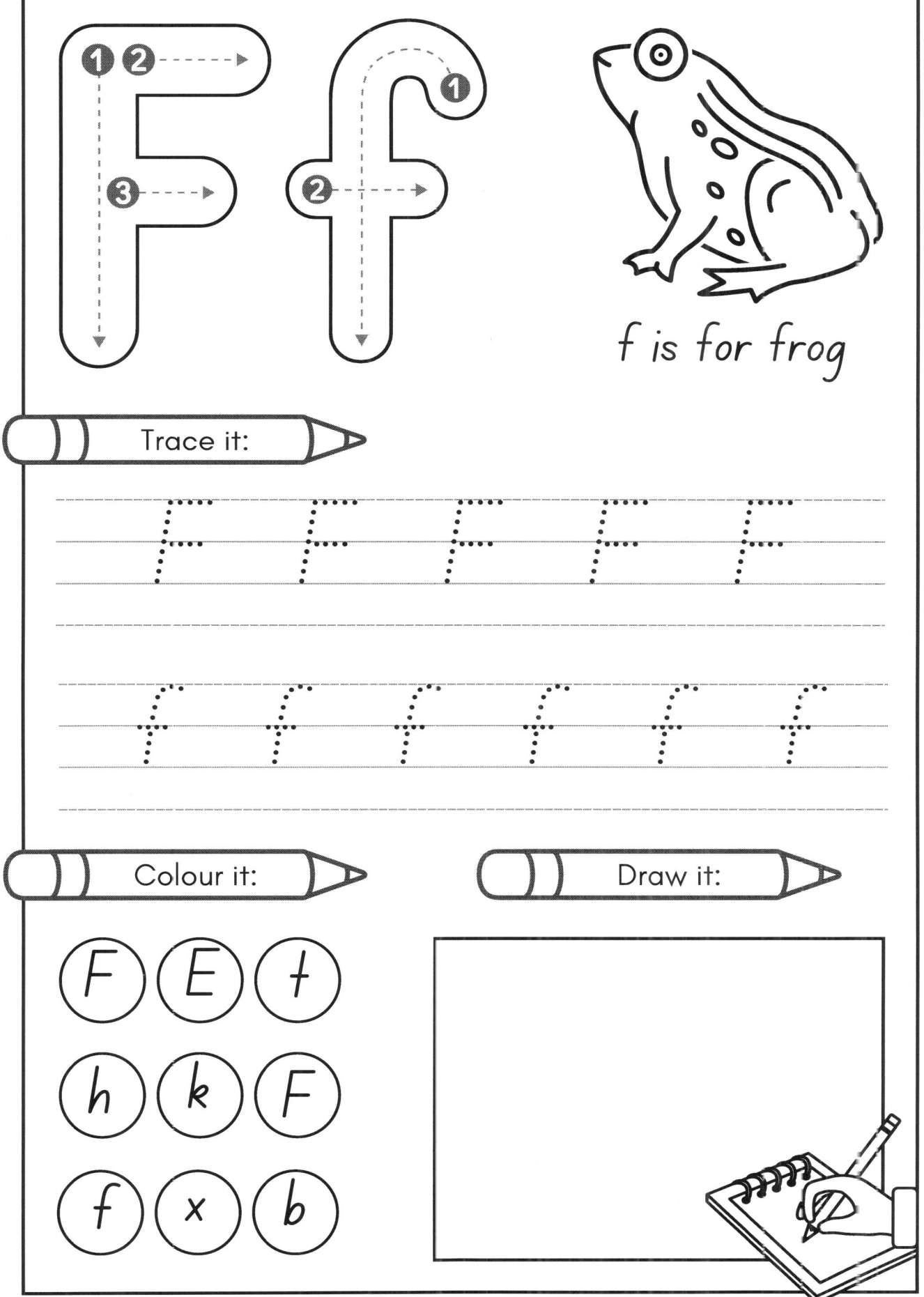

f is for frog

Trace it:

F F F F F

f f f f f

Colour it:

F E t

h k F

f x b

Draw it:

Gg

g is for goat

Trace it:

G G G G G G

g g g g g g

Colour it:

(p) (g) (y)

(j) (G) (Q)

(q) (m) (y)

Draw it:

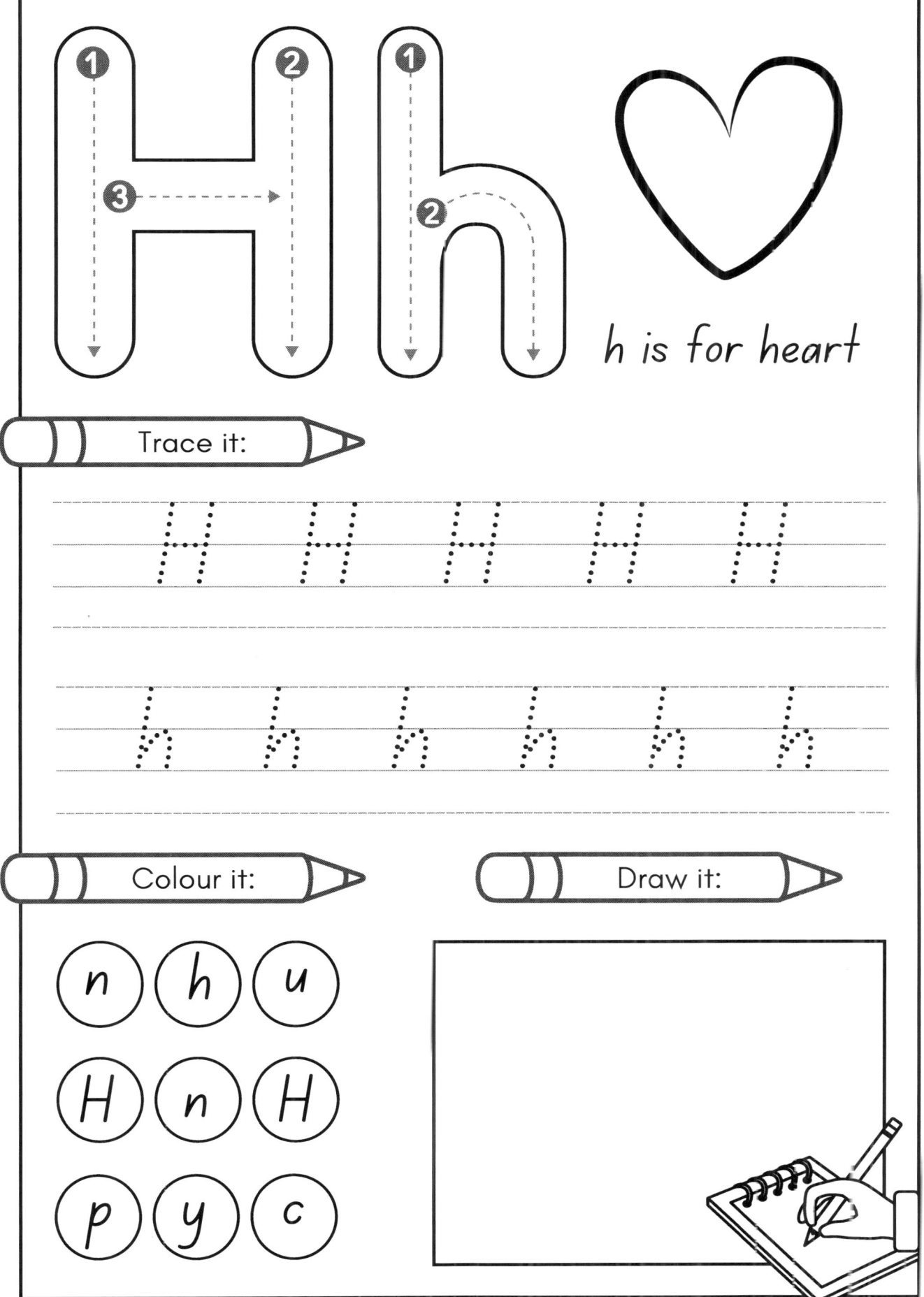

h is for heart

Trace it:

H   H   H   H   H

h   h   h   h   h

Colour it:

(n) (h) (u)

(H) (n) (H)

(p) (y) (c)

Draw it:

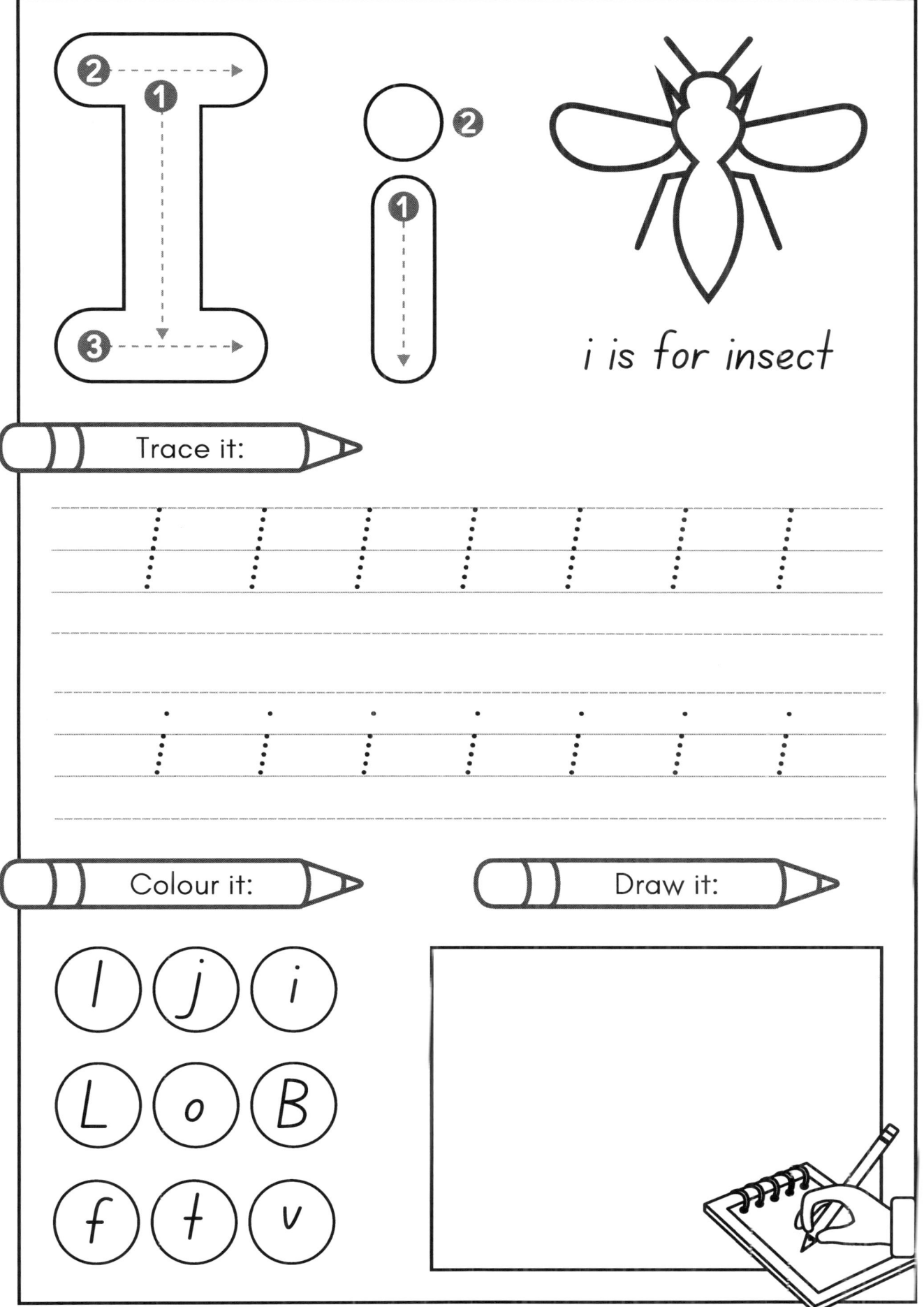

i is for insect

Trace it:

Colour it:

Draw it:

J j

j is for joey

Trace it:

Colour it:

Draw it:

K k

k is for koala

Trace it:

K K K K K

k k k k k k

Colour it:

k K r

R t S

y m w

Draw it:

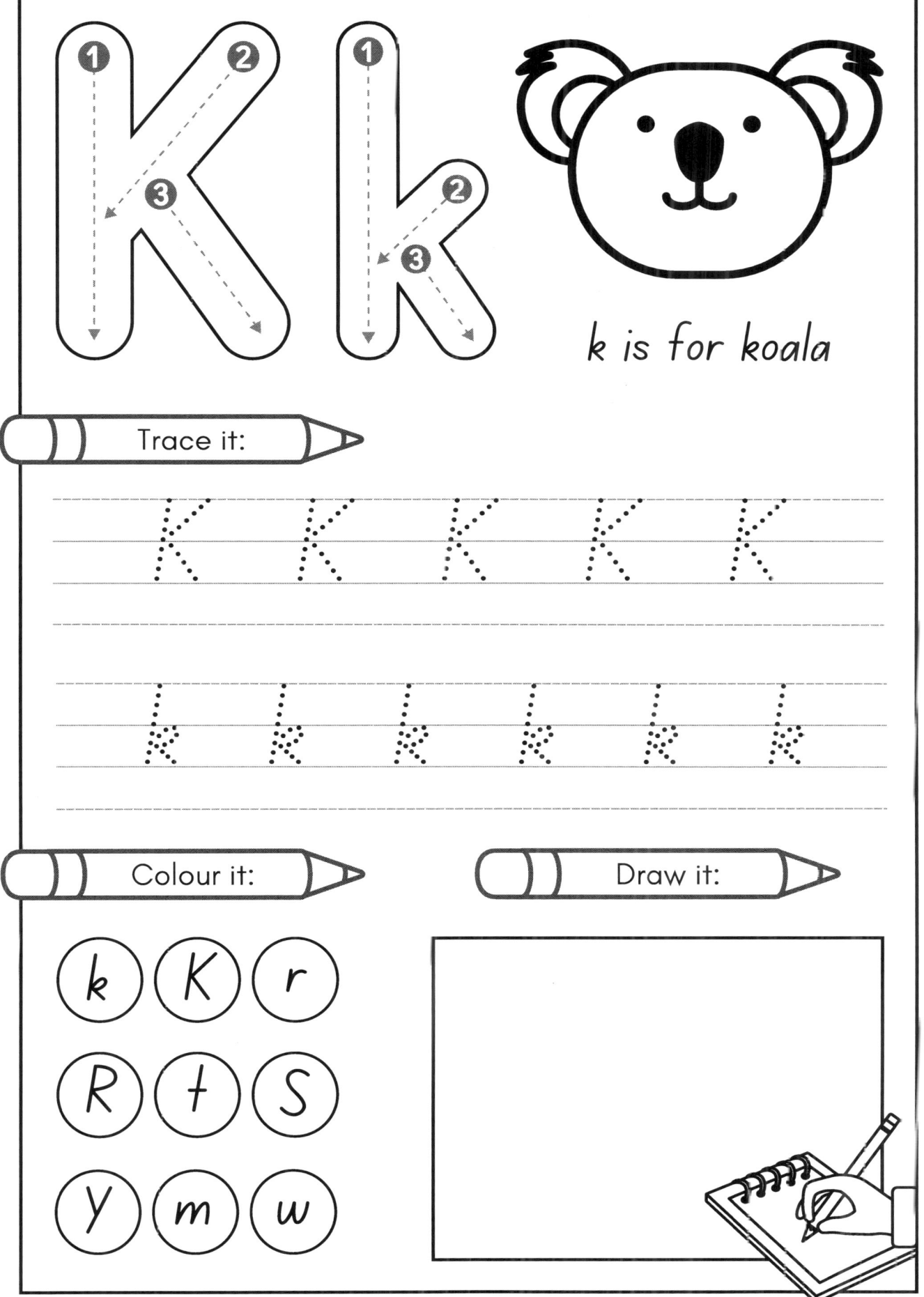

l is for lemon

Trace it:

Colour it:

Draw it:

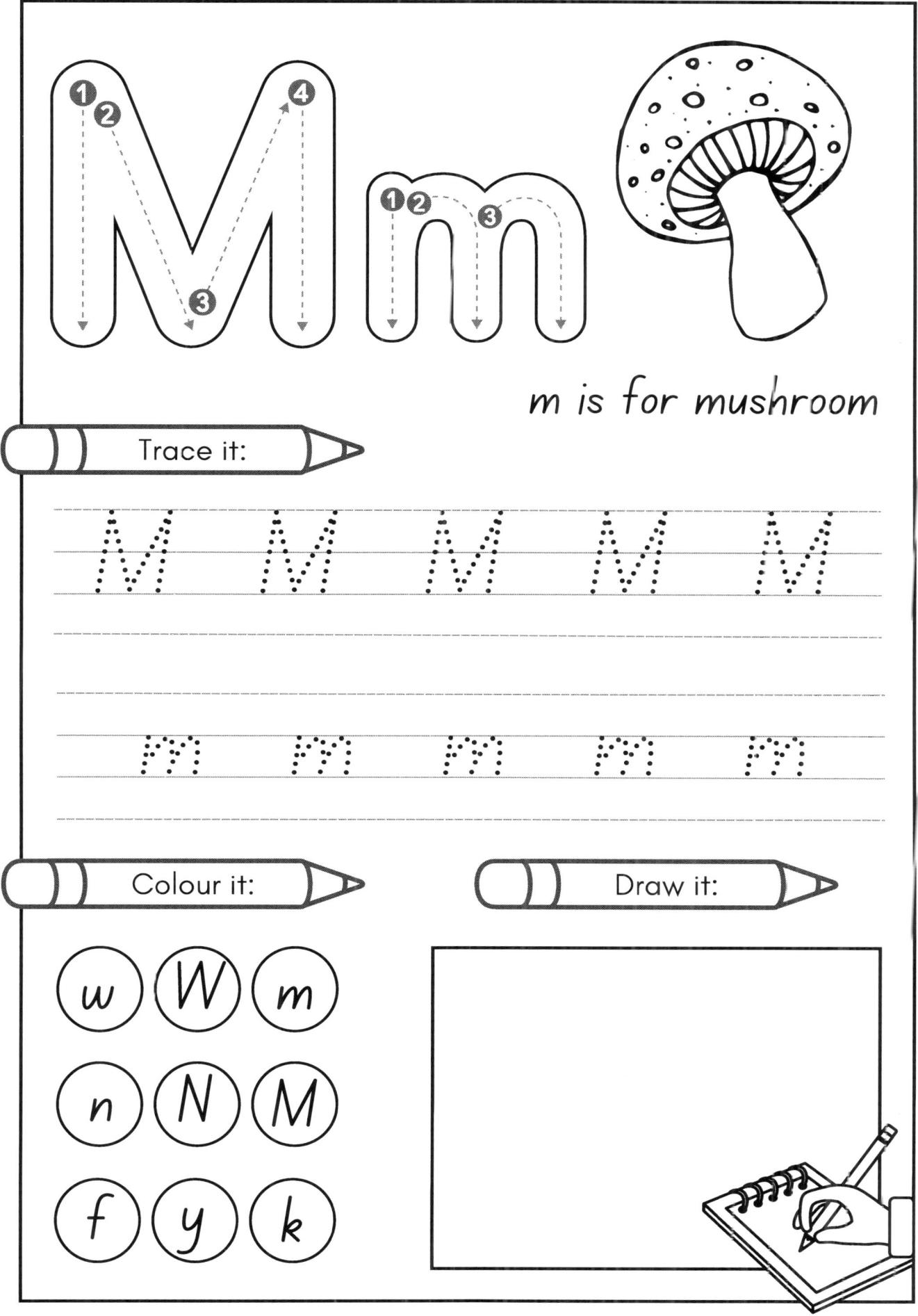

M m

m is for mushroom

Trace it:

M M M M M

m m m m m

Colour it:

w W m

n N M

f y k

Draw it:

Nn

n is for net

Trace it:

N N N N N

n n n n n

Colour it:

j b d

t n M

N z a

Draw it:

o is for octopus

Trace it:

O   O   O   O   O   O

o   o   o   o   o   o

Colour it:

O   h   o
b   g   L
x   e   u

Draw it:

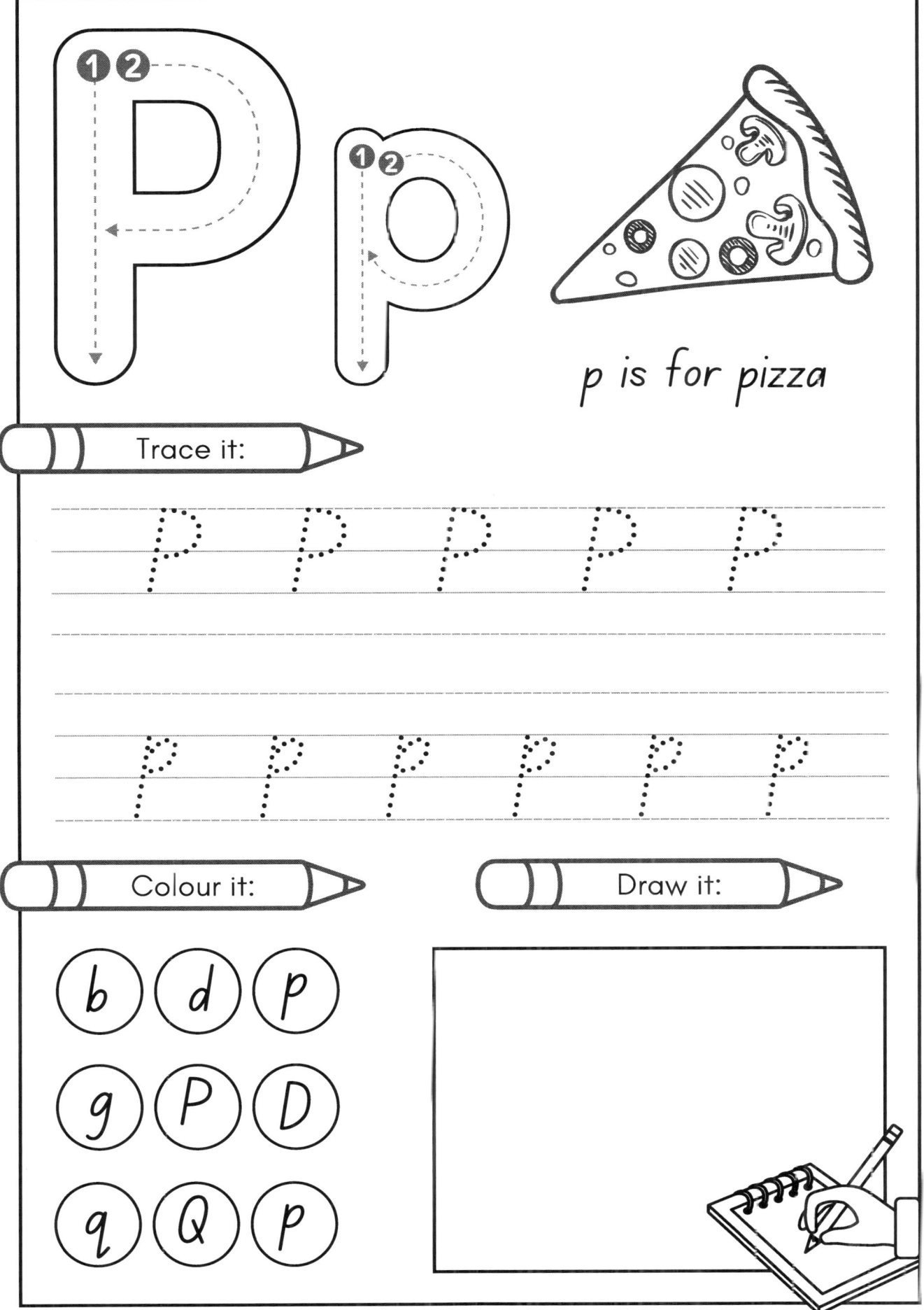

P p

p is for pizza

Trace it:

P P P P P

P P P P P

Colour it:

b d p

g P D

q Q P

Draw it:

q is for queen

Trace it:

Q Q Q Q Q Q

q q q q q q

Colour it:

g Q q

j y D

d b q

Draw it:

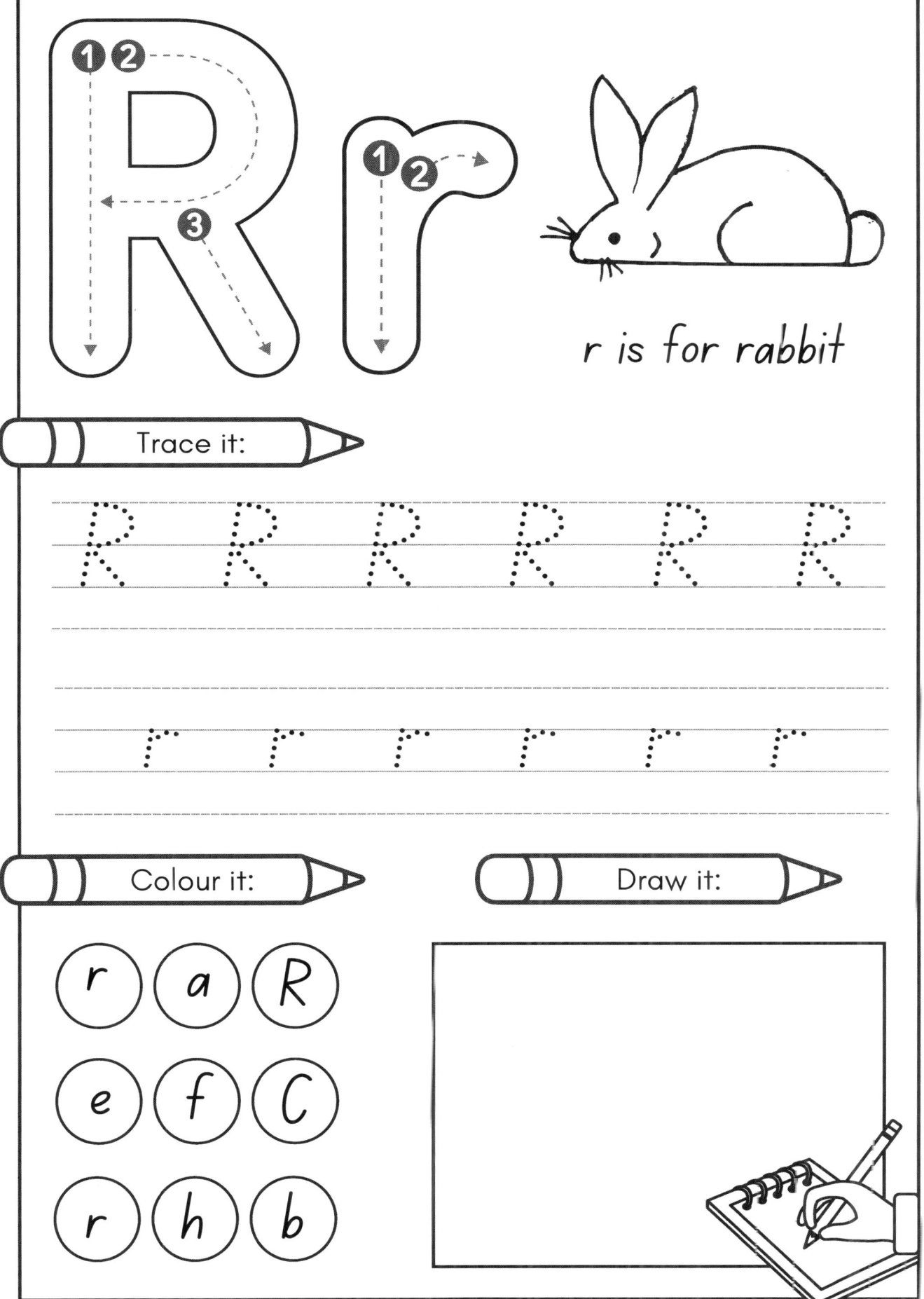

r is for rabbit

Trace it:

R R R R R R

r r r r r r

Colour it:

Draw it:

r a R

e f C

r h b

S s

s is for sun

Trace it:

S S S S S

s s s s s s

Colour it:

d f s

s c H

S y q

Draw it:

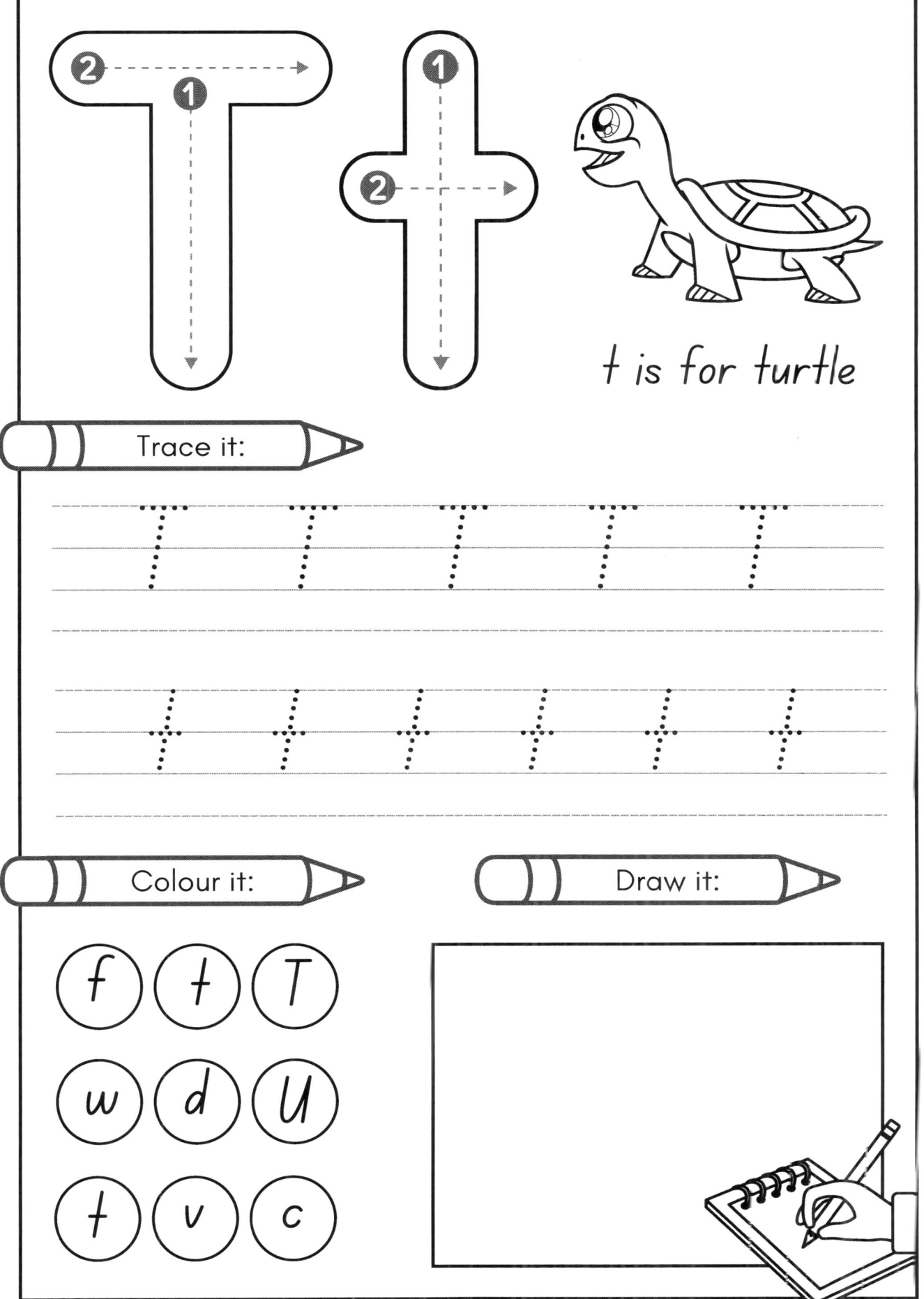

t is for turtle

Trace it:

Colour it:

Draw it:

f t T

w d U

t v c

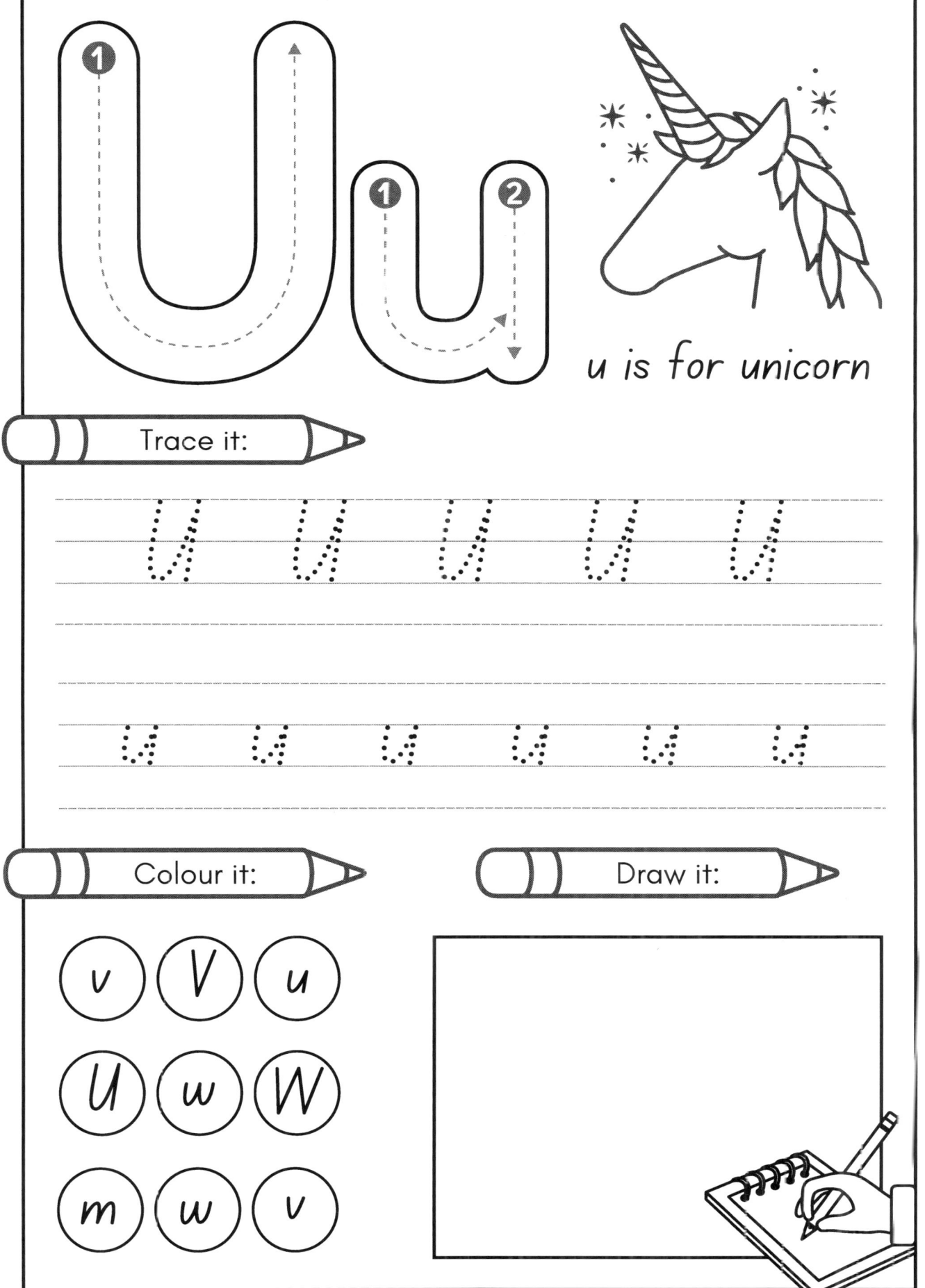

U u

u is for unicorn

Trace it:

U U U U U

u u u u u u

Colour it:

(v) (V) (u)

(U) (w) (W)

(m) (w) (v)

Draw it:

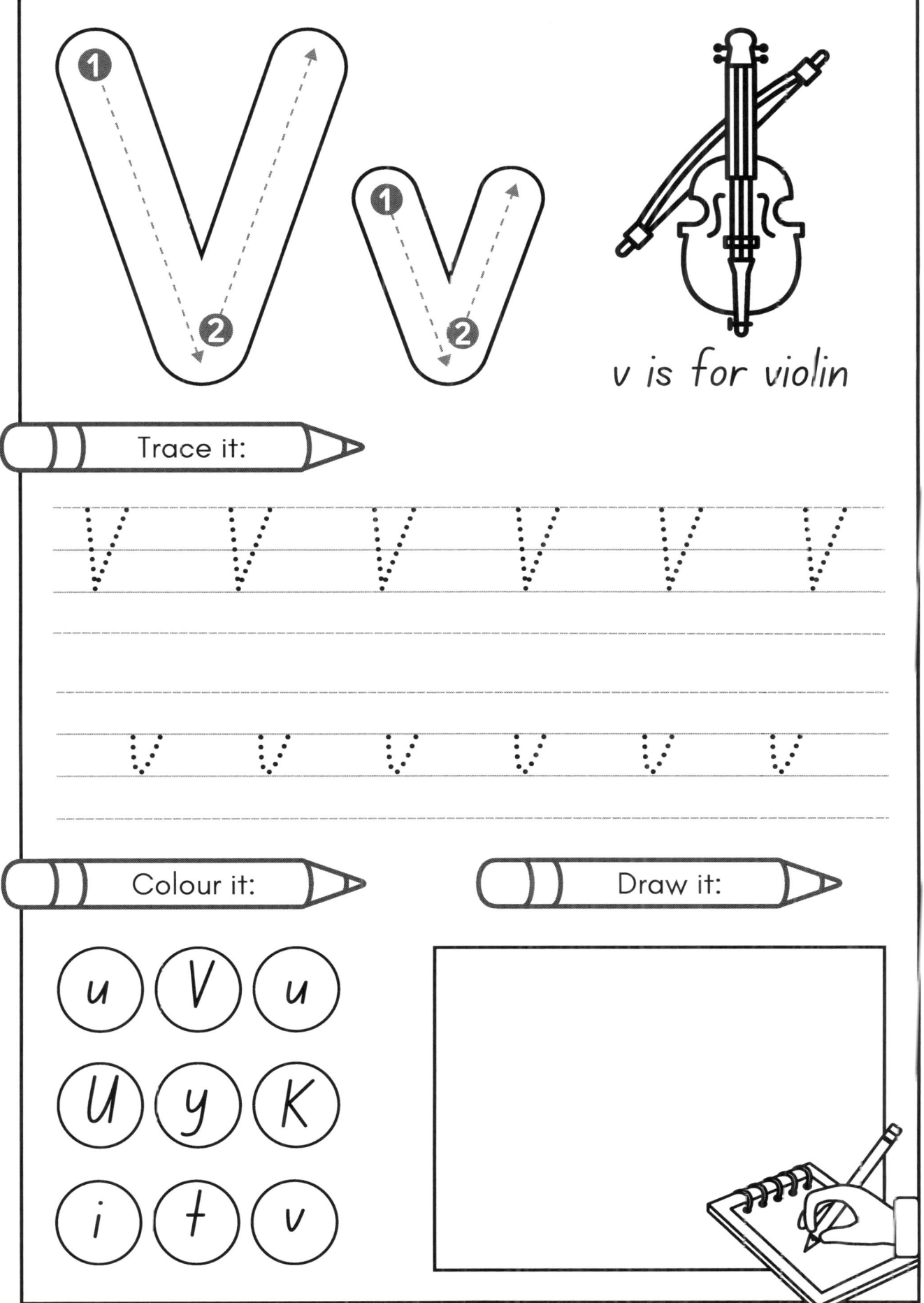

v is for violin

Trace it:

Colour it:

Draw it:

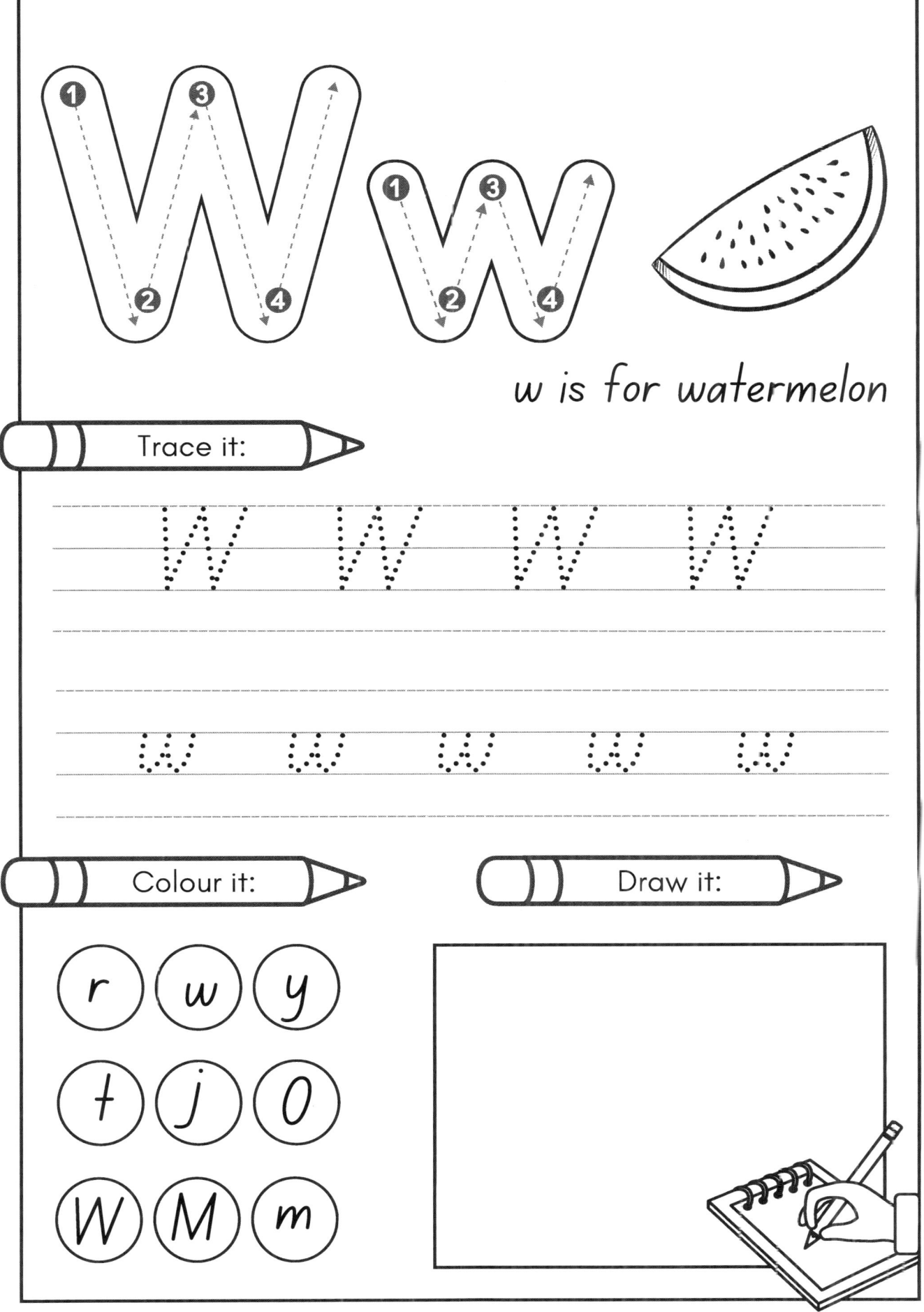

w is for watermelon

Trace it:

Colour it:

Draw it:

x is for x-ray

Trace it:

X   X   X   X   X

X   X   X   X   X   X

Colour it:

t   X   T

s   x   G

h   Z   X

Draw it:

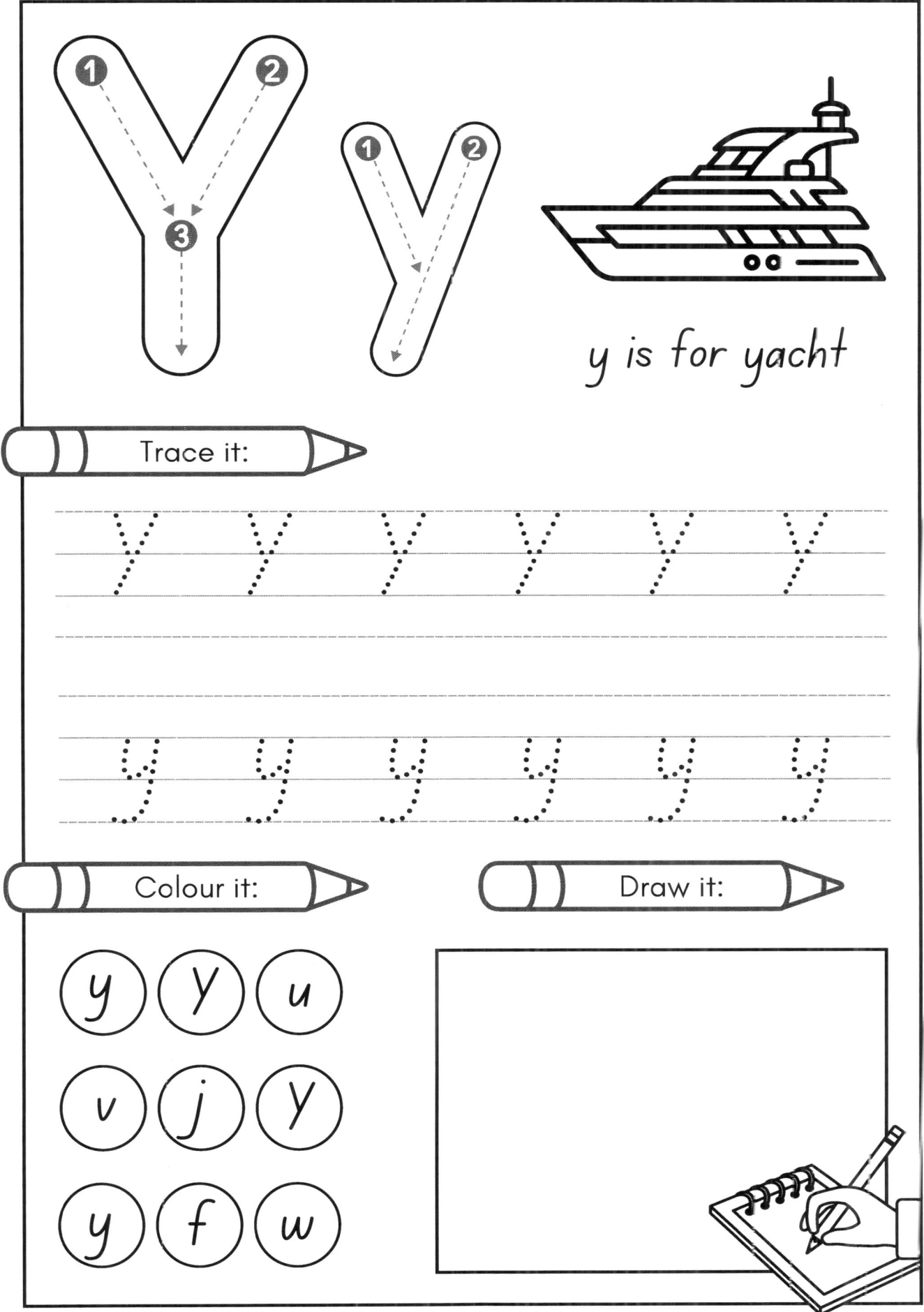

y is for yacht

Trace it:

Colour it:

Draw it:

z is for zebra

Trace it:

Colour it:

(s) (Z) (z)

(u) (t) (R)

(Z) (S) (X)

Draw it:

Color

Color

Airplane

Circle it!

A B Z G U U B Y G
K A Y A P B A A

Color the pictures with the letter sound.

Color

B

Color

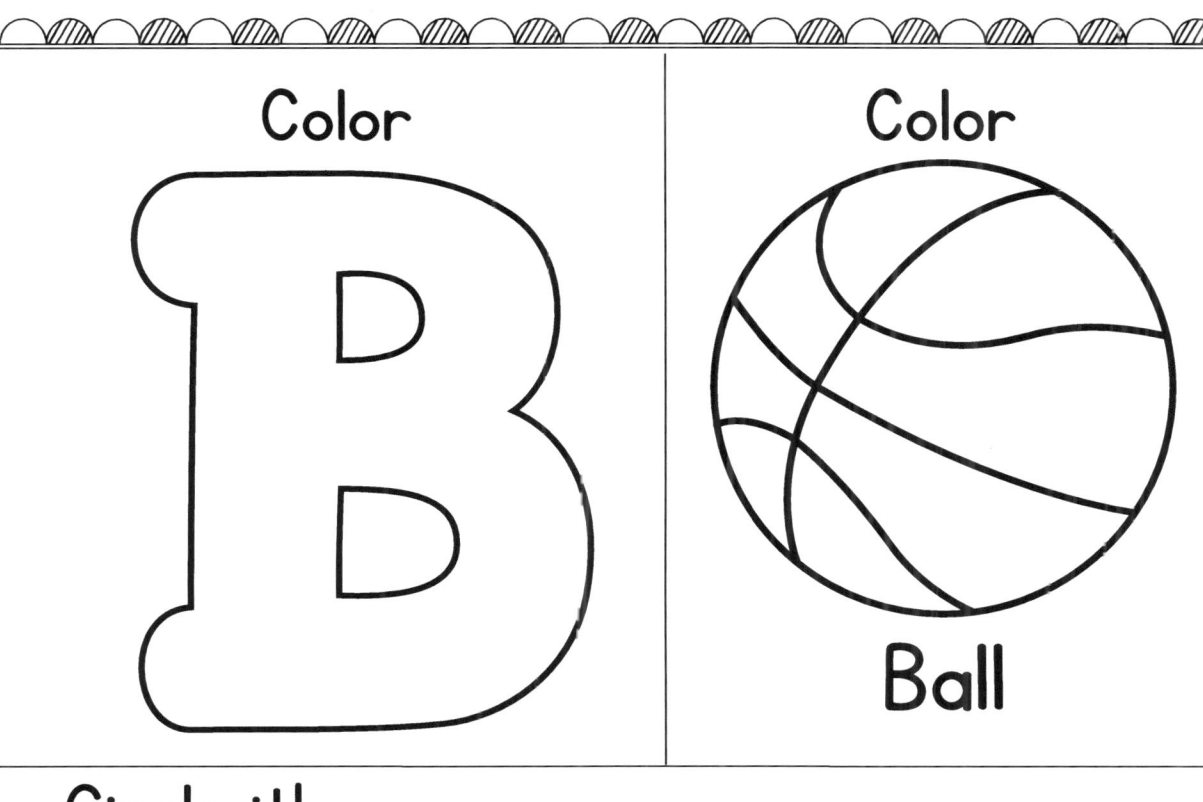

Ball

Circle it!

S B Z V B M H
G U A Y
K B X O B B L B

Color the pictures with the letter sound.

Color

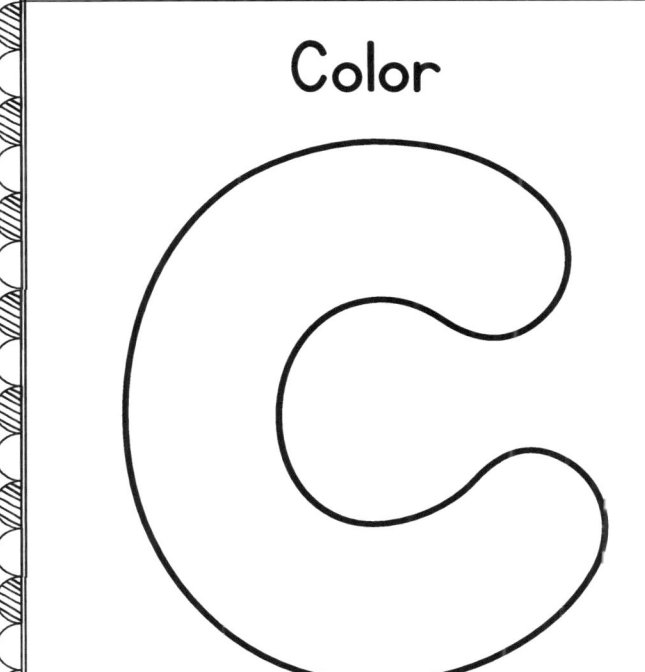

Color

Cat

Circle it!

C A Z G C J M
C L A C
C X S C F C K
R S

Color the pictures with the letter sound.

Color

Color

D

Doll

Circle it!

D R Z X D G Y D
U L
K D H A T D M D

Color the pictures with the letter sound.

Color

E

Color

Elephant

Circle it!

Q E Z T E O B E I X
K E P A E O R H E E

Color the pictures with the letter sound.

Color

Color

Fish

Circle it!

F E Z N B Y H

G U F F

F A S D F Z F R

Color the pictures with the letter sound.

Color

G

Color

Giraffe

Circle it!

G G Z G C Y X
G F V G
W Z A G M G B
G

Color the pictures with the letter sound.

Color

Color

House

Circle it!

H A H F O K L M
B X H D J C N
H O H
H

Color the pictures with the letter sound.

Color

Color

Igloo

Circle it!

I F I I D I M G I
  D U
I A H I J K I L
        I   N

Color the pictures with the letter sound.

ink

Color

Color

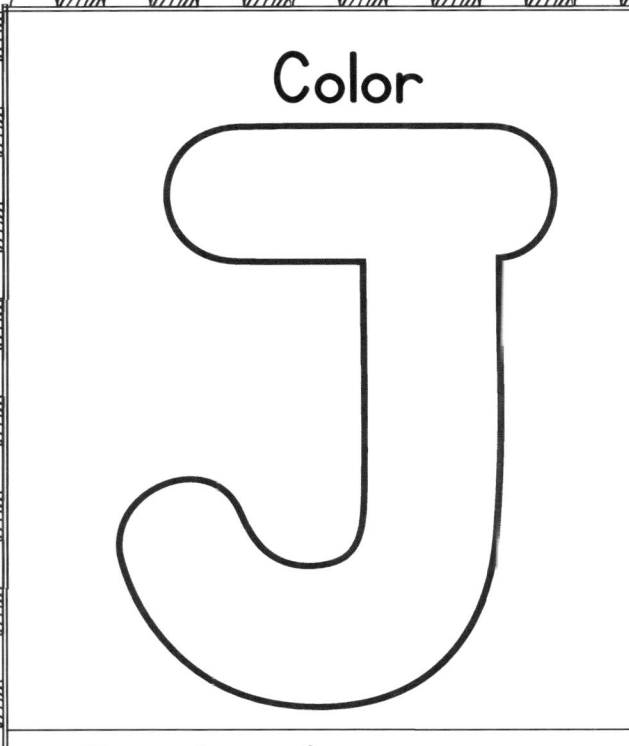

Juice

Circle it!

J W Z O J J E X
K Q P J I
  J R T A J

Color the pictures with the letter sound.

Color

K

Color

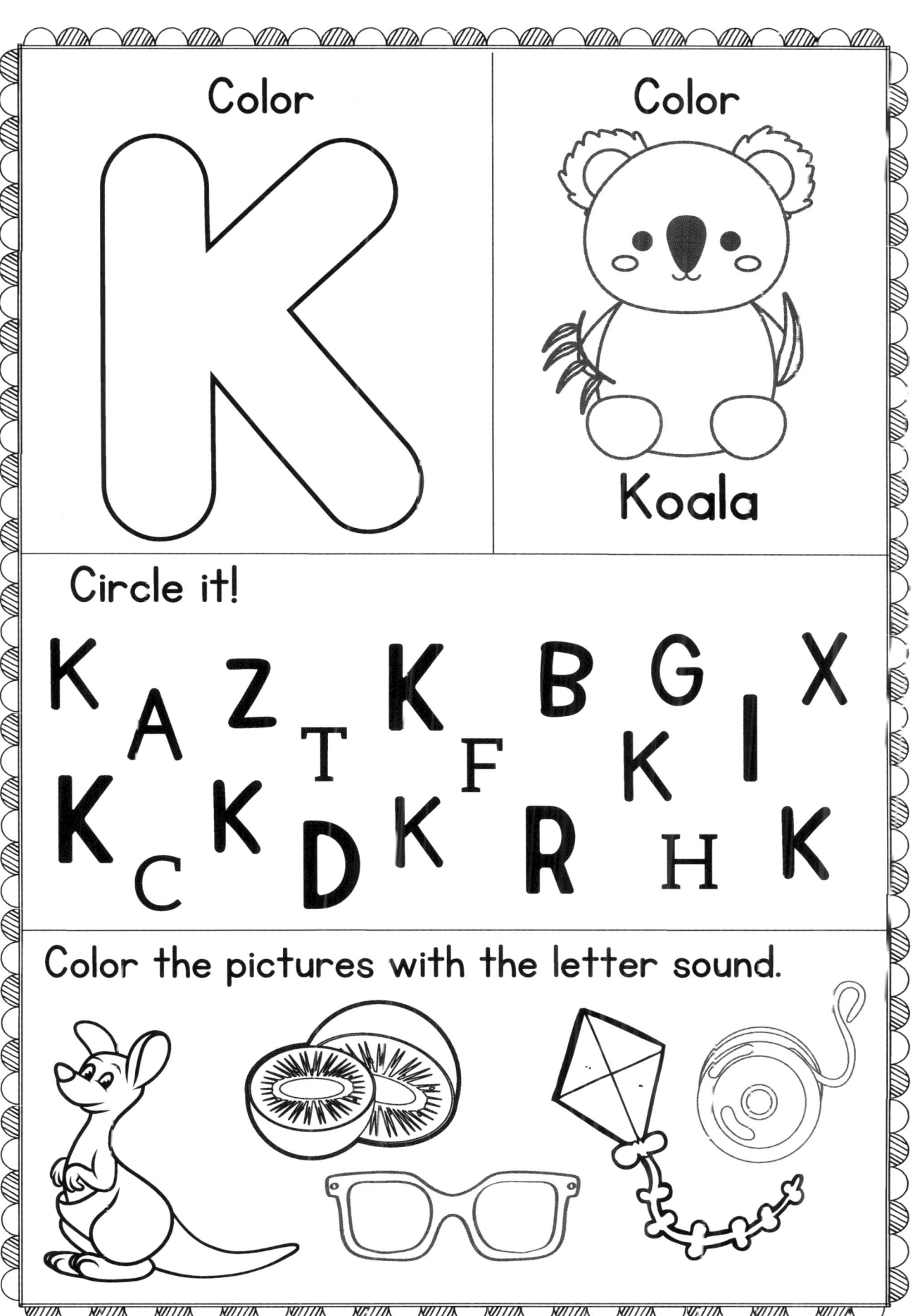

Koala

Circle it!

K A Z T K B G X
K K T F K I
K C D K R H K

Color the pictures with the letter sound.

Color

Color

Lion

Circle it!

A L Z L L D L
K L B M L L G N
   L B L C R L F

Color the pictures with the letter sound.

Color

M

Color

Moon

Circle it!

M A C D M X G
K M M W S M
E V E T M J

Color the pictures with the letter sound.

Color

N

Color

Notebook

Circle it!

V A N L M W C
N J M L W N K
O N E Q H J

Color the pictures with the letter sound.

Color

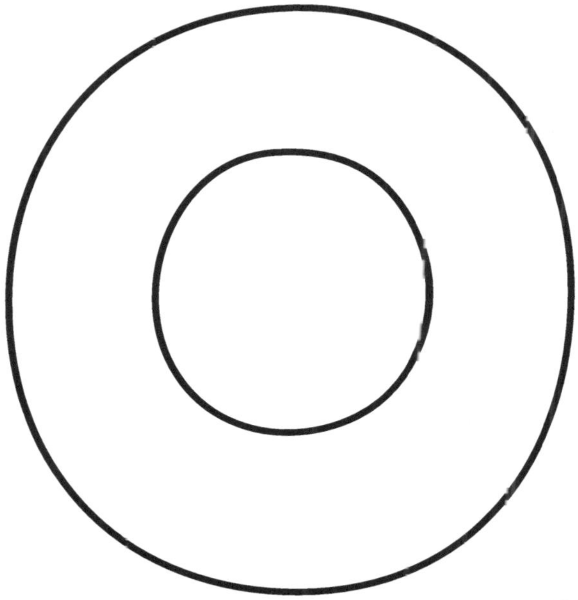

Color

Octupus

Circle it!

P O A O T Y G
Z E O M W S O
  O V O B L J

Color the pictures with the letter sound.

Color

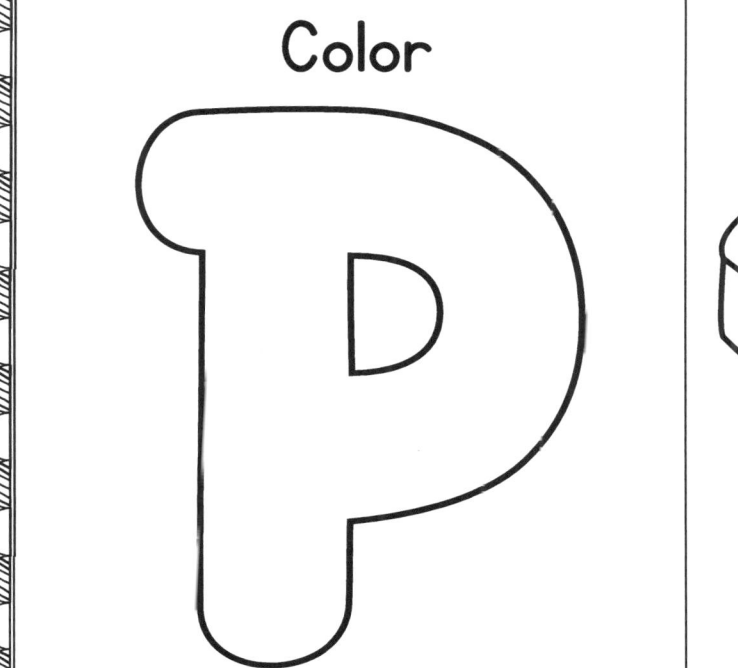

Color

Piano

Circle it!

P O J O D Y U

M P C S P
H
P R A V L T

Color the pictures with the letter sound.

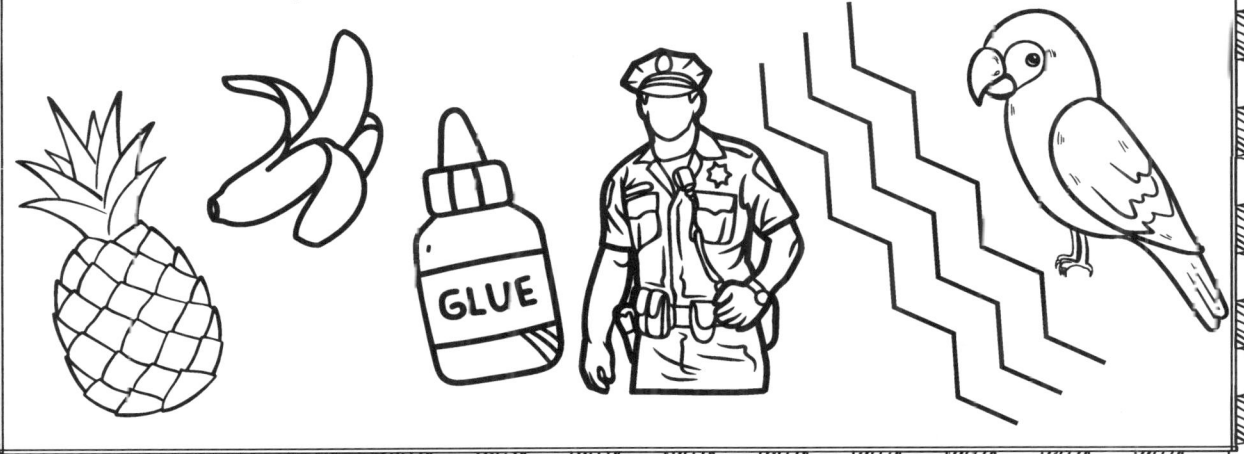

GLUE

Color

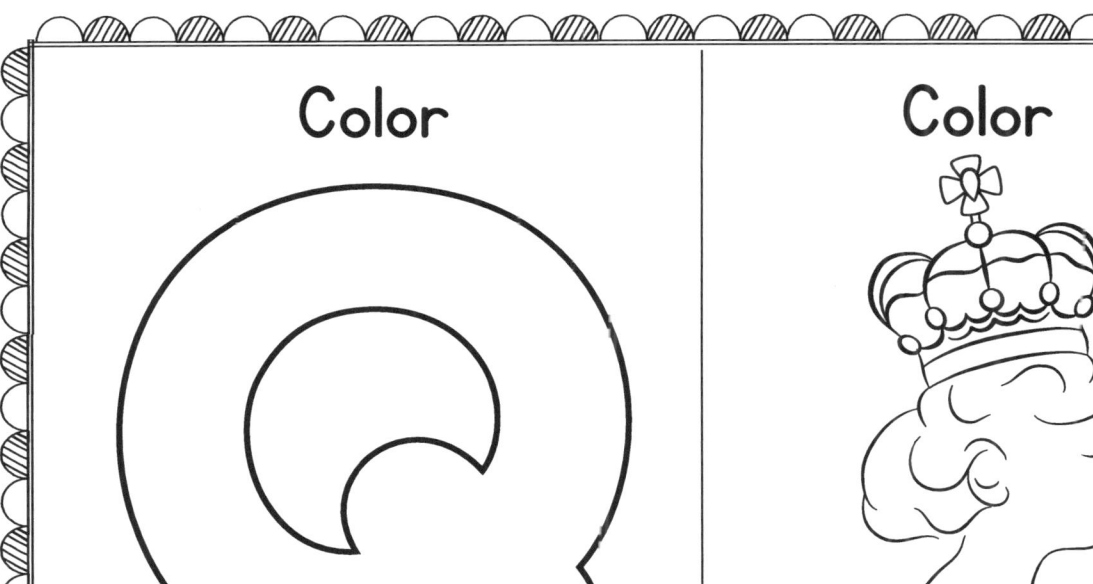

Color

Queen

Circle it!

W O B S Q Z Y X

I E Q S U Q Q

L E N P Z

Color the pictures with the letter sound.

Color

Color

R

Raccoon

Circle it!

X O Q R H Y A
 R A L G W
 I S R E O R C

Color the pictures with the letter sound.

Color

Color

Seahorse

Circle it!

K R J S H T F
X P A E S N
S H G D R B

Color the pictures with the letter sound.

Color

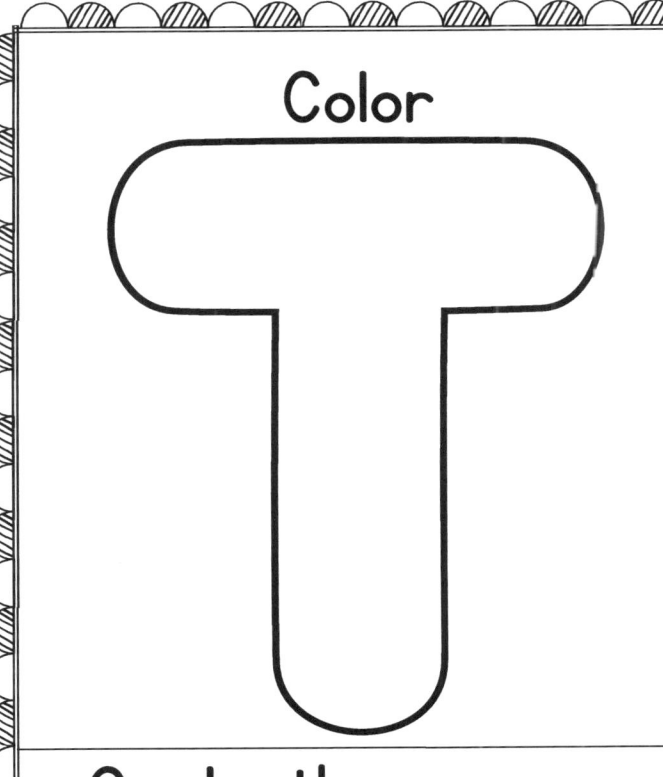

Color

Tiger

Circle it!

T R F O H D E

Q A T L N

H T U G D R X

Color the pictures with the letter sound.

Color

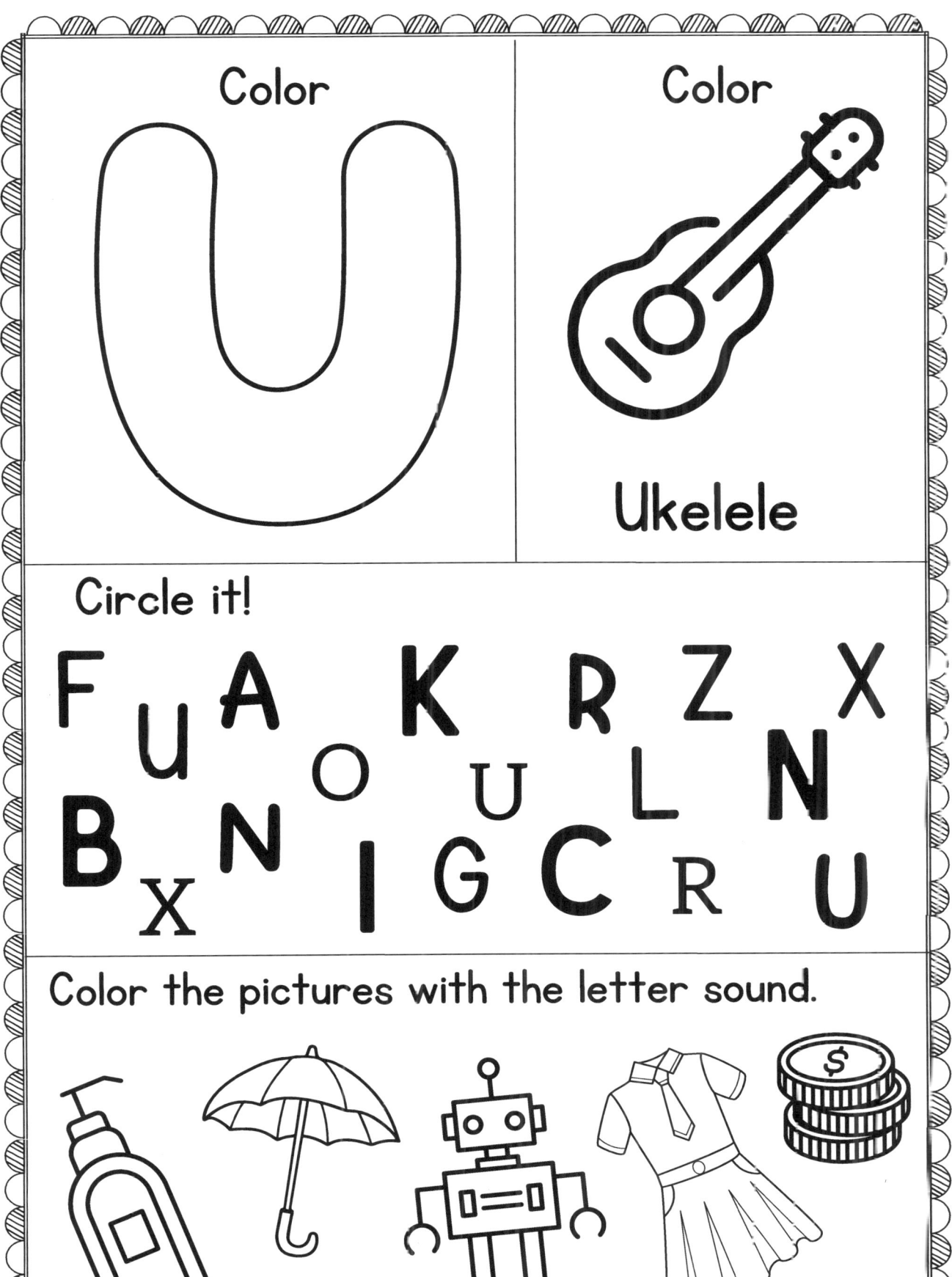

Color

Ukelele

Circle it!

F u A K R Z X
B N O U L N
X I G C R U

Color the pictures with the letter sound.

Color

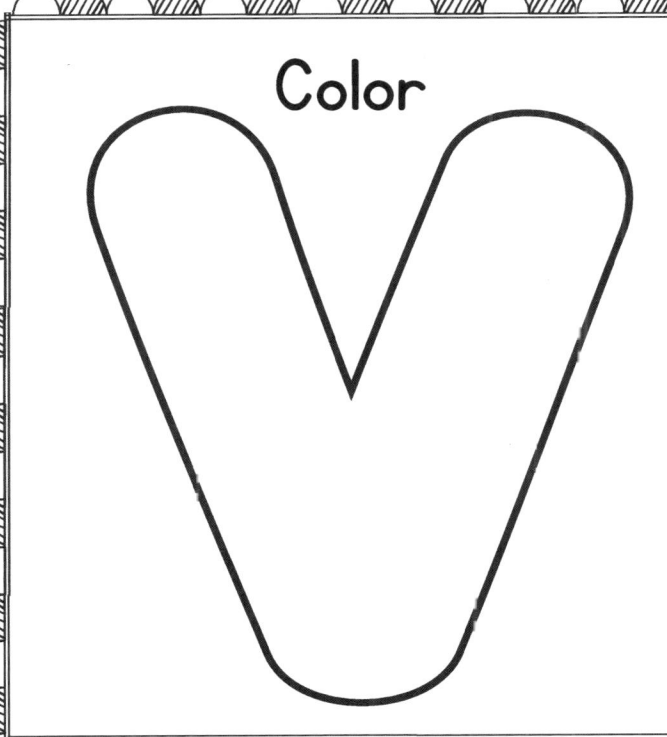

Color

Vacuum

Circle it!

V   A   S   V   X   T
L
M   V   S   B   L   R
H   K   G   D   P   R   Z

Color the pictures with the letter sound.

Color

Color

W

Wheelchair

Circle it!

G F W C Z X U
N K B S M K
W L I W T A

Color the pictures with the letter sound.

Color

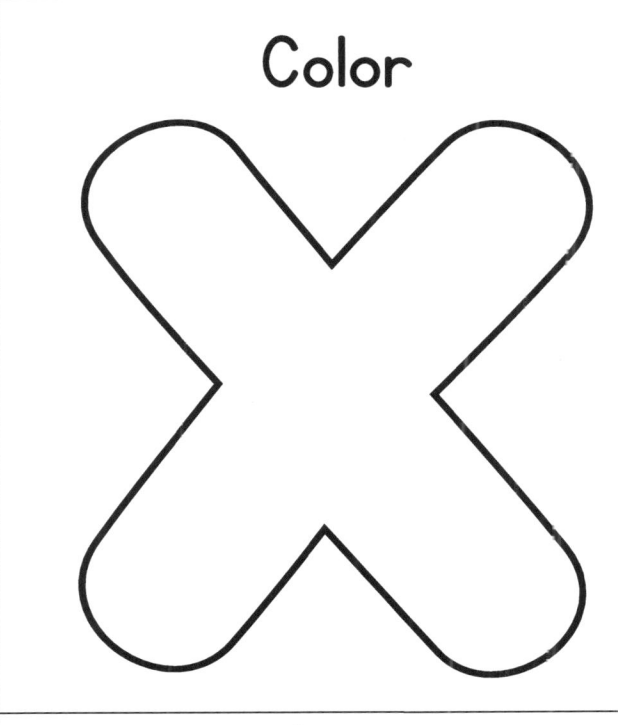

Color

Xenops

Circle it!

C P N F S T F
M U
X M X
B V P I W X B

Color the pictures with the letter sound.

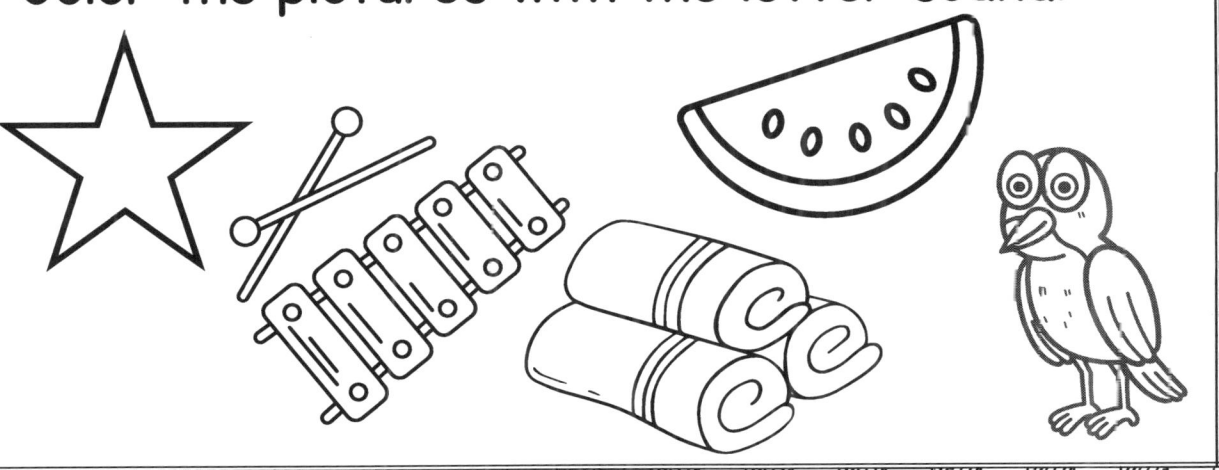

Color

Color

Yacht

Circle it!

X A G L Y H I
J K O E M T
Y C Q Y Z Y

Color the pictures with the letter sound.

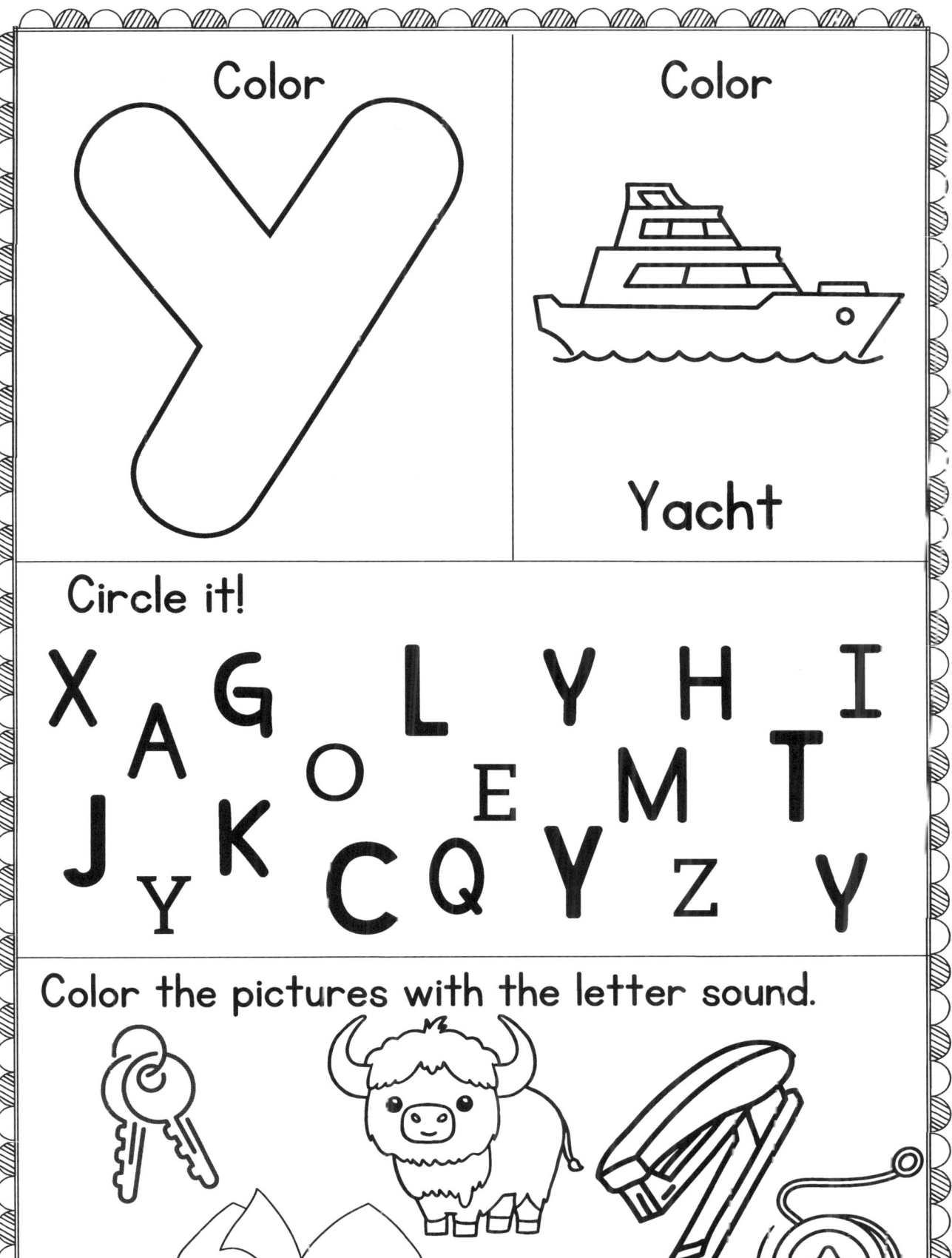

Color

Z

Color

Zipper

Circle it!

Z B L V Z S J
K N P U F G
Z W X Y Z H

Color the pictures with the letter sound.

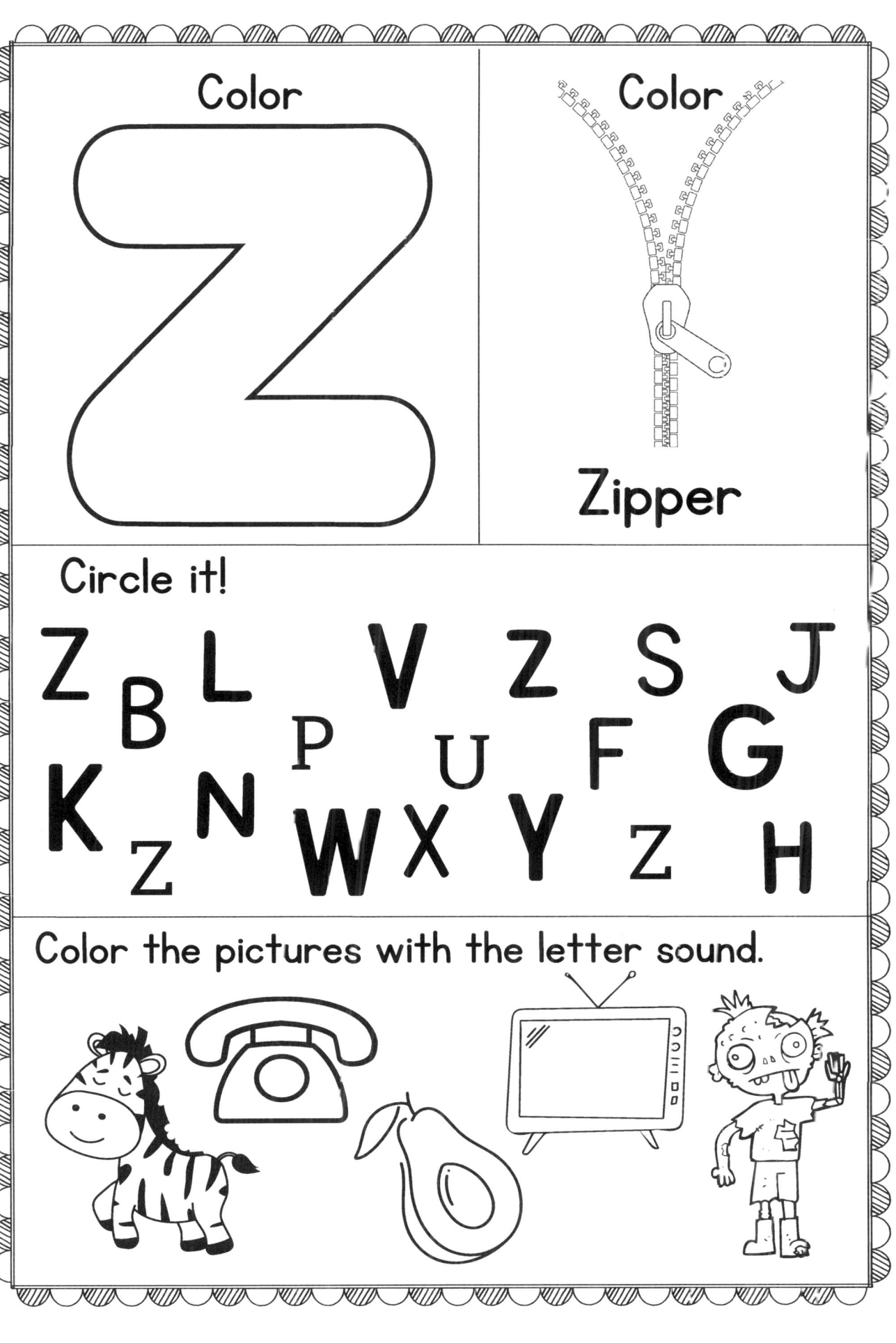

Letter Aa

Trace letter Aa. Then color the pictures that begin with letter A.

The Letter Bb

Trace letter Bb. Then color the pictures that begin with letter B.

The Letter Cc

Trace letter Cc. Then color the pictures that begin with letter C.

The Letter Dd

Trace letter Dd. Then color the pictures that begin with letter D.

The Letter Ee

Trace letter Ee. Then color the pictures that begin with letter E.

The Letter Ff

Trace letter Ff. Then color the pictures that begin with letter F.

The Letter Gg

Trace letter Gg. Then color the pictures that begin with letter G.

The Letter Hh

Trace letter Hh. Then color the pictures that begin with letter H.

The Letter Ii

Trace letter Ii. Then color the pictures that begin with letter I.

The Letter Jj

Trace letter Jj. Then color the pictures that begin with letter J.

The Letter Kk

Trace letter Kk. Then color the pictures that begin with letter K.

The Letter Ll

Trace letter Ll. Then color the pictures that begin with letter L.

The Letter Mm

Trace letter Mm. Then color the pictures that begin with letter M.

The Letter Nn

Trace letter Mm. Then color the pictures that begin with letter M.

The Letter Oo

Trace letter Oo. Then color the pictures that begin with letter O.

The Letter Pp

Trace letter Pp. Then color the pictures that begin with letter P.

The Letter Qq

Trace letter Qq. Then color the pictures that begin with letter Q.

The Letter Rr

Trace letter Rr. Then color the pictures that begin with letter R.

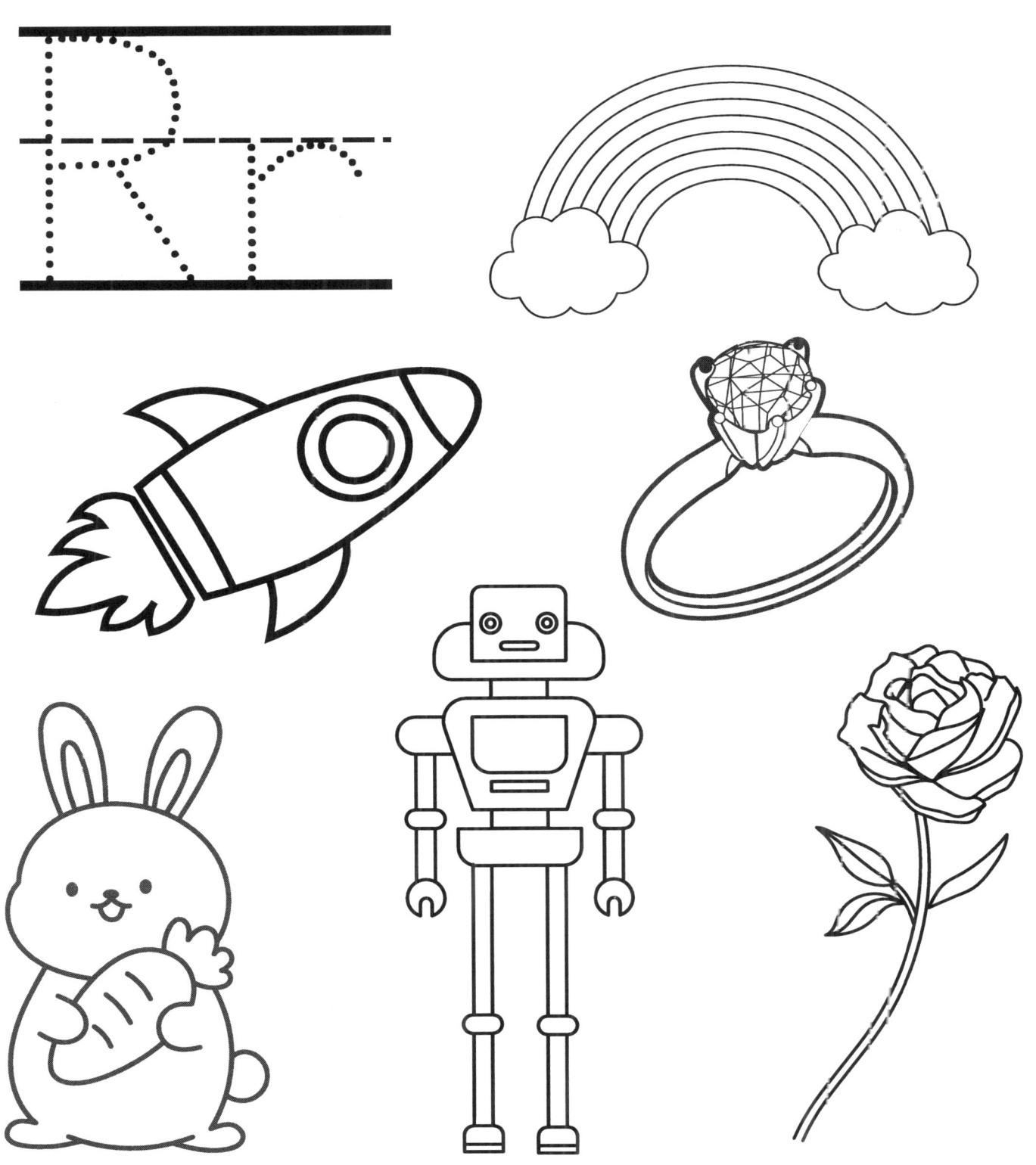

The Letter Ss

Trace letter Ss. Then color the pictures that begin with letter S.

The Letter Tt

Trace letter Tt. Then color the pictures that begin with letter T.

The Letter Uu

Trace letter Uu. Then color the pictures that begin with letter U.

The Letter Vv

Trace letter Vv. Then color the pictures that begin with letter V.

The Letter Ww

Trace letter Ww. Then color the pictures that begin with letter W.

The Letter Xx

Trace letter Xx. Then color the pictures that begin with letter X.

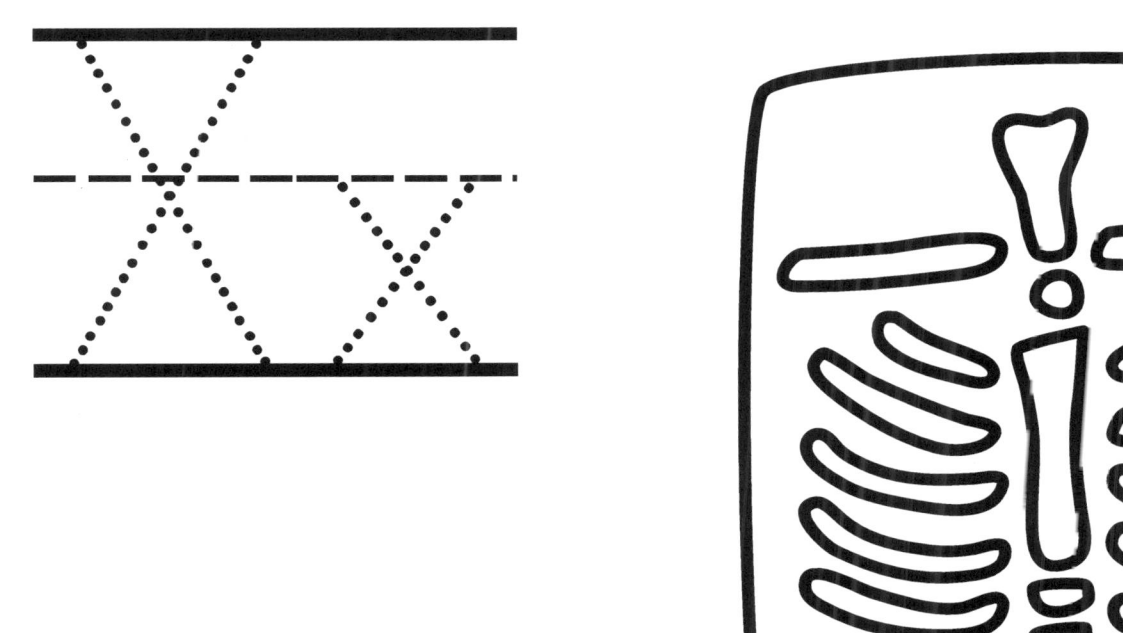

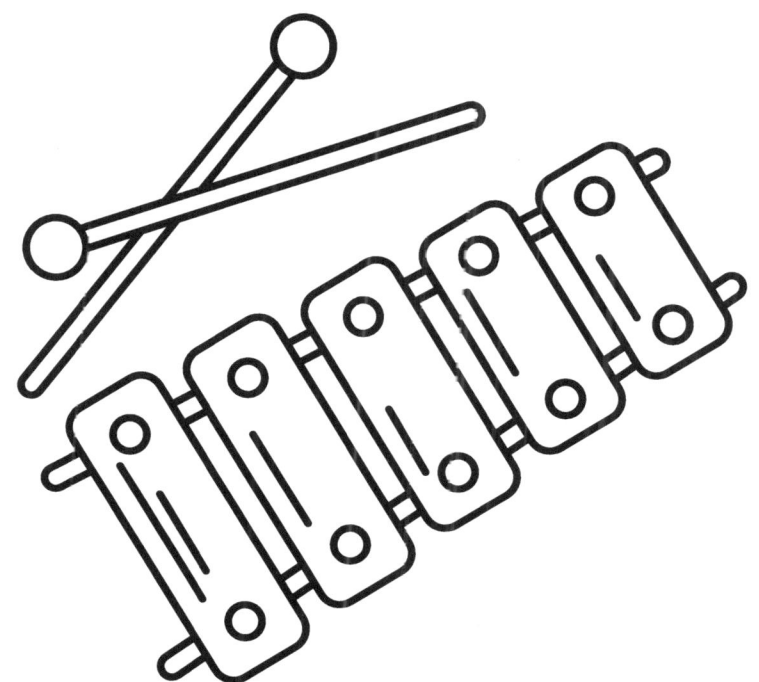

The Letter Yy

Trace letter Yy. Then color the pictures that begin with letter Y.

The Letter Zz

Trace letter Zz. Then color the pictures that begin with letter Z.

Made in the USA
Middletown, DE
14 August 2025